MW00354118

bless it

Reflections from a Pandemic

Kate Buckley • *Author*
Teresa Lacks • *Illustrator*

KBB

PUBLISHING

GEORGIA

For you —

the one cracking open this book.

May these words and sketches speak to
something within you.

And may they bless you.

ISBN 978-0-578-76803-8

First edition October 2020.

Library of Congress: 2020918472

Cover Design by David Provolo

Printed in the USA.

KBB

PUBLISHING

Georgia

Table of Contents by First Line

blessed be the ones covered with cloth

aprons and masks

packaging the peas and potatoes

with gloves and care

for the stranger at checkout

whose eyes

radiate everything

blessed be the backyard gardeners

elbow deep in therapeutic mulch

pushing the wet earth

and the wet earth pushing

headlines to the sidelines

for a brief reprieve

to smell the roses

blessed be the fall

dormancy begins per usual

relief from the hectic buzzing and sweltering

but gusts from tropical depressions

usher us into a different flavor of autumn

one with maybe football

maybe school

maybe worship

definitely God

blessed be the vistas

sprawled across horizon lines

vibrant with steadfast magnificence

but freshly alive to newly opened eyes

transmitting life, color, bounty

and calm

blessed be the back-pew Presbyterians

displaced for a moment or an eon

attempting solace on a screen

trusting in tomorrow

a wooden bench warmed again

blessed be the parent

facing the fall

send to school or teach from home

balancing worry + safety + science + social

crunching the factors of sanitizer and friends

swirling angst and fraying nerves

may it all be well

blessed be the graduates

hanging in midair

like the cap and tassel

they would have tossed in fanfare

sliding through skipped transitions

and blurred chapters of life

moving on to the unknown

of the future

and grasping for ways to mark

achievements of the past

blessed be the workforce

faced with an impossible choice

that feels like no choice at all

grinding out of bed

to grind the coffee beans

to grind *others'* coffee beans

for the double espresso to-go

blessed be the siblings

together 3,029 hours and counting

squabbles and cranky moods

Monopoly marathons

charades and fort-building

words they did not mean

in a tone they did not intend

followed by hugs they did not want to give

but contagious smiles and giggles

they could not stifle for long

blessed be the ones working from home

dishes piling in the sink

toddlers racing through the living room

zoom meetings with unmuted mics

the stress of too many jobs at once

guilt that none gets the attention it deserves

blessed be the human

fickle, flawed

indivisible from its past

woven together in beauty and tragedy

a product of its setting

negotiating its birthplace with

every moment that comes after

solidly justified blindness or

earth-shattering potential

it is time to be brave

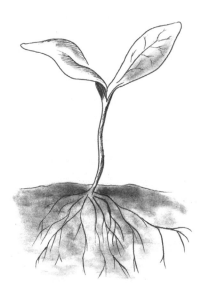

blessed be the at-home gym

constructed with makeshift parts

on the garage floor

absorbing all the extra

that doesn't know how to fit

inside our beating chest

accepting every bit of sweat

until we are tired enough

to rest

blessed be the decision maker

losing sleep

over how to walk the line

between alarmists and deniers

seeking to guide with confidence

but also humble flexibility

exhausted by the dance

and overwhelmed by the weight

yet bolstered by the thought

of precious hearts

blessed be the sound

of pen scratching paper

crisp and productive

as we try to put words to the wordless

jotting down the way it is

when it isn't like anything before

a memo-rial to the weirdness

and the hardship of distance

may our words be a scaffold

reaching across, however skeletal, to connect

blessed be the breeze

that snags the loose hair

until it billows out in mayhem

giving up the act

of seeming put-together

bursting from buttoned-up

into confidently mussed

free to be

blessed be the one on the bridge

calm one moment

unnerved the next

trying with all his might to glimpse

the other side

that sits in mystery, blurry fog

hiding the view

he has only here and now

the bountiful now

blessed be the mommas

scurrying to all the places

scrolling through all the feeds

running in place long after the workout

throwing productivity

in the face of the unease

hoping to distract themselves

from the scary undercurrent of

living in limbo

blessed be the business owner

holding tightly to the strained seams

using themselves to close the bursting gap

boosting morale with the team

balancing the checkbook by lamplight

stressing about PPPs and loan documents

wishing there was just more time

more money

more certainty

and a little more hope

blessed be the new baby

unaware & fresh

sheltered and cuddled and held

swaddled in tenderness

by ones whose love is bigger than

they knew it could be

birthing hope

for a new day

blessed be the lonely

stuck in sameness

bored of the view

waiting for the phone to ring

watching the seasons change

through the window

daring to look inwards

to find the hope they couldn't see

by looking out

blessed be the friend

who walks outside

so she can hear you crying

who says, "it won't always be this way"

and tells you that you're never alone

so you can hitch up your pants

tighten your boots

and get back to growing up

with renewed fervor

blessed be the sensitive

who feel with rawness the relentless news

who tense under the weight

of the world

who wonder if maybe

they are at capacity

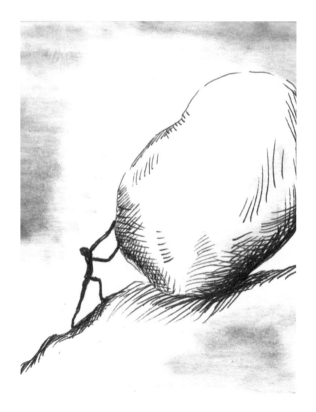

blessed be the tears that flow

in streams of nomadic grief

forced underground

and under masks

sadness that cannot be shared

or absorbed by the touch of loved ones

may they water the parched patches of now

hydrating a life-giving tomorrow

blessed be the choir member

missing the weight of the robe

the cloak of friendship

the vibrations of shared melodies

humming a solitary strain

until hymnal harmonies happen again

blessed be the ones who notice

a need

showing up with an open heart

a bag of groceries

a prescription re-fill

a twinkle in the eye

a bottle of sanitizer

packaged in hope

and delivered to the doorstep

blessed be the sidewalks and trails

a playground

for the cooped-up

the air-conditioned

the self-absorbed

opening themselves up to be ridden upon,

trodden down and run all over

for the sake of fresh air & sane minds

blessed be the ones whose faces throb

indented with mask lines

feet swollen from standing in the hospital room

and trekking the fluorescent halls

scrubs laundered over and over

and over again

all so they can care for the lungs

that threaten to shut down

in room. after room. after room.

blessed be the teachers

cherishing inquisitive minds

classrooms prepped and

smelling of pencil shavings

but this year

holding another layer

on top of the scholastic usual

heavy with worry and

laminated protocols

blessed be the drifting

unmoored between

familiar past and unknown future

...

the job that ended suddenly

and the one yet to be discovered

...

well-worn routines

and startling new shores

blessed be the soil

rich with infinite particles of life

grounding us as we scurry

churning the remnants of death

into fertile freshness

crumbling, shifting, changing

absorbing it all

and cradling endless possibilities

in its sodden embrace

blessed be the sleepless

bodies horizontal

but minds frantic

racing and spinning

with thoughts too large

and worries too dark

...

there aren't enough sheep

blessed be the one

whose lifeline of connection

is a white rectangle on the kitchen table

alien in its portals and dings and home buttons

who can see the video

but there is no sound!

whose brow furrows

at error messages

or thwarted

downloads, buffering, swiping

blessed be grands

parents + children

separated by decades and households

by countries, states, or miles

aching for the perfumed hug

the applesauce-sticky hand-holding

the shriek at the punchline of the favorite book

long overdue

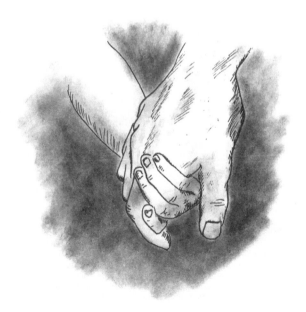

blessed be the counselors

lending exhausted ears

to variations on a theme

mitigating despair

watching train wrecks in slow motion

hopeful that a well-timed phrase

might find a fertile groove

towards healing

blessed be the bank account

dwindling too quickly

notifications with red ink

startlingly off-kilter

losing its balance

faltering

shuffling for solid footing

fortitude feels far off

blessed be the mirror

that watches the face

before the pretense

or the toothpaste

or the concealer

and absorbs + reflects

all that it sees, no choice

but to tell the truth

blessed be the broken

hobbling along

some days throbbing drudgery

spirits in shambles

mirroring the fractures of the body

other days peppier and lighter

wholeness on the horizon

one foot.

then another.

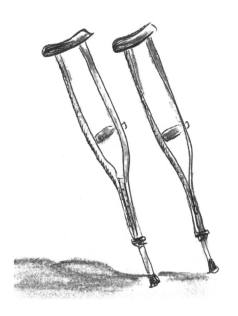

blessed be the families

rubber bands stretched to the max

each connected to the other

in a web of tight tetherings

spring-loaded

ready and waiting to bounce

as ammunition

or resilience

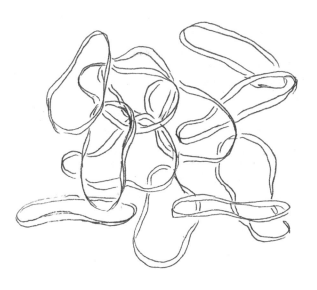

blessed be the peaches

watching it all unfold

perched on the counter

ripening into prime sweetness

oblivious to the goings-on in the kitchen

the snide comments thrown in haste at 7am

the slap-happy laughter

when the day is done

and so is mom

blessed be the one

overwhelmed by spinning plates

patchworking childcare

juggling laundry and night shifts

fretting about the cost of it all

on the wallet & on the blood pressure

terrified to pause too long

for fear that one may drop

and shatter

blessed be the rain

arriving in cozy sheets of serenity

to cover the tin roof

soaking the grass

squeals from the umbrella-less children

announce the baptizing

of everything

showers that replenish

blessed be the friction

the coarse scraping

the caustic scratches

required to yield a spark

for the slow burn

to warm the constricted

vessels of the system -

the jolt needed for survival

blessed be the times

when the ballot box

provokes the tissue box

a vote goes in

with a heavy heart

a kleenex comes out

to blot away the tears

everything feels like it's falling

blessed be the ones

struck by a stick or a stone

rubble from the un-aimed explosion

of someone's top blowing

nicked by the debris that was

hurled in frustration

at circumstance

tattooing those on the periphery

with scars and grudges

blessed be the authenticity

timid and wandering

masquerading as 2D entertainment

pronouncing that the #photooftheday

is #lookgoodfeelgood with #nofilter –

a #happy #selfie because #lifeisgood

if only real life

could be so #organic and #blessed

blessed be the ministers

fielding frustrated phone calls

filming, editing, re-filming

praying through windows & from driveways

tempering their own panic

to exude a calm they do not feel

comforting the sick from a distance,

the distance sickening

relying on God in a wi-fi wilderness

and leaning into the not-yet

blessed be the Meyers lemon

morphing into yellow juiciness

inching closer

one day at a time

to its fullest potential

its brightest glow

tangy aroma & pine earth pucker

hanging on

thriving

blessed be the ones

hungry for the familiar

crackly loaf + Welch's grape juice

on white cotton linens

draped over the mahogany table

in the middle of the sanctuary

snacking on manna in the wilderness

making do with crumbs

that are enough

blessed be the memories

of backyard games with friends

four square and

slip – n – slides

are slipping into photo albums

and sliding into "back in the day"

sweet times in sepia print

remember when… high fives were ok

and hugs were as natural

as Southern lemonade

blessed be the coffee maker

sounding like exhaust brakes

revving up to drip a cup of warmth

the kitchen swirling

with nutty, bold brew

pouring gusto with a pinch of sugar

to face the day

and all it will bring

blessed be the first

on the scene

hearts reeling and clamoring with the sirens

ready as they will ever be

to bandage the wound

to compress the chest

to raise the ladder to the window

muttering a tired prayer beneath their breath

that this one might live

blessed be the sick

with lungs that wheeze

eyelids that burn

hearts that race

and bodies that throb

with the gravity

of tomorrow

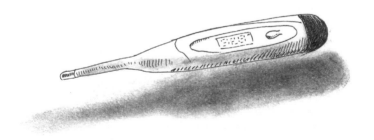

blessed be the laughter

that bubbles up uninvited

taking away the breath

for a nanosecond of mirth

leaving an afterglow of fullness

a sigh of gratitude

that we didn't forget

how it feels to lose ourselves

to joy

blessed be the unraveling

pulled to desperate tautness

by incessant stress

wondering how long it'll hold

tiring of the wait

amazed at the tenacity

of its own fibers

blessed be the ones

practiced in the art of stillness

who dare to dwell

on a mat or a cushion

flowing or grounded for

a cycle of breaths

the reminder that

we are

blessed be the post

flag perked up

alert and expectant

eager to house a handwritten scrawl

delivering

a sign of life from the town over

a note sealed by a human tongue

a bridge from that kitchen to this one

blessed be the space

suspended between then and soon

seemingly frozen

as the world spins around it

hovering in pause

pregnant with the unsung

blessed be the student

excited anticipation of a brand-new grade

gently packing the pristine crayons &

unblemished notebooks

right next to the cheerfully bright masks

which barely cover

the angst and the worry

of parentless hallways

and shortened recess -

blessed be the concentric circles

rippling out from their center

the nucleus of the crisis

the drop that started the movement

they cannot help but to widen

and broaden

and reach out

and out and even farther out

leaving no piece of the whole

untouched

or unmoved

blessed be the trees

swaying in the breeze

bending to the changing winds

shaping themselves to the new and unfamiliar

yet with foundation unwavering

roots spread out wide and deep

showing us how to be

blessed be the festive table

set with love and care

missing a few seats this year

a screen propped up next to the gravy bowl

beaming in big smiles

thankful for this day

no matter what

blessed be the marriage

navigating the cratered road

swerving potholes of fatigue and strain

puttering on fumes

laboring up a hill

then the shock of the downward slope

noticing the glint off the pavement

the exhilaration of wind in the hair

the joy of the foot pressed to the floor

committed to adventure

what a ride.

blessed be the internet memes

forwarded, pinged, texted, and tweeted

creatively crafted

tragic hilarity

resonating across oceans

and going viral

to the stunned and forlorn who are

aching to laugh

blessed be the hand stretched out

in greeting

an imprinted habit of goodwill

left un-held

un-shaken

met only with a cringe

at the potential hazard of connection

what do we do now

blessed be the season

smelling of fir needles scattered on the floor

like snow blanketing the ground

house windows like torches casting

a soft, warm glow

holly berry wreaths the celebratory sentinels to

a small, quiet Christmas

kind of like that first silent night

muted.

anticlimactic.

miraculous.

blessed be the one

tender from the probing ultrasound wand

stinging from the painfully familiar news

the charts, the beeps, the pills, the shots

the counting, the doing, the waiting

a tired routine that breeds

finely-tuned fury at baby bumps everywhere

barely hidden panic

desperate sighs of surrender

she dares to cling to a narrative all her own

may her cramps give birth to promise

this time

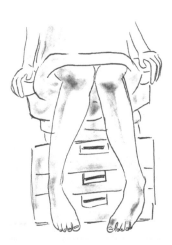

blessed be the couple

when the save-the-date is

struck through and re-sent

the venue is closed indefinitely

the reception size is pared down

and whose love

shines through the n95s

unfazed

blessed be the light

peeking out from behind the clouds

in brave beams

pointing to the truth

that no storm cloud

lasts forever

blessed be the day

when the child is grown

and she looks in the rearview

to find a story to tell the little ones

and she remembers the time

when everything stopped

and hung there

and it was terrible and heartbreaking

and it was fertile and vibrant

and the whole world had a chance

to sort priorities and to choose

what matters most

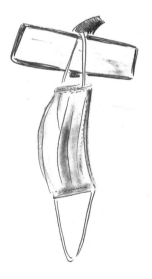

Acknowledgments

Shout-out to DOWNTOWN CHURCH in Columbia, South Carolina. Their "blessing" cards sparked the idea for these written poems of blessing.

Thank you to the many who edited the words, design, and arrangement of these blessings: Dr. Leslie Fuller, Ada Owens, and Dr. William P. Brown.

TERESA LACKS • *Illustrator*

Teresa was born and raised in Raleigh, North Carolina. She currently works as a School Psychologist in the Boston area. Teresa combines psychology and visual art to help children with unique learning styles explore their self-concepts, take risks, and process   emotions in healthy and creative ways. She graduated from Davidson College with a degree in Studio Art in 2015 before attending Tufts University, where she obtained her Master of Arts/Educational Specialist degree in 2020.

KATE BUCKLEY • *Author*

Kate started writing books on little steno pads at age five. At the University of Georgia, she earned her degree from Grady School of Journalism. She got her Masters of Divinity from Columbia Theological Seminary in Decatur, Georgia. Now Kate lives on the coast of Georgia with her husband, Stuart. She is "Mom" to three children and serves as the Parish Associate at St. Simons Presbyterian Church. *Bless It* is her first book. It is a compilation of bite-sized verses that name some of the challenges of the Covid pandemic - couched in blessing and wrapped in love.

photo by @elizawarnerphoto